Papyrus of the Pillow

Luca WM Blood

chipmunkapublishing
the mental health publisher

All rights reserved, no part of this publication may be reproduced by any means, electronic, mechanical photocopying, documentary, film or in any other format without prior written permission of the publisher.

Published by
Chipmunkapublishing
PO Box 6872
Brentwood
Essex CM13 1ZT
United Kingdom

http://www.chipmunkapublishing.com

Copyright © Luca W.M. Blood 2011

Edited by Martine Daniel

Chipmunkapublishing gratefully acknowledge the support of Arts Council England.

Author Biography

Luca is diagnosed with schizo-feria as he likes to call it, and later described as co-morbid personality ,During his first so-called- brain-breakdown, I described what I heard, saw and felt, as pixilation energy and began to sense spiritual activity, living as a kind of modern-day hermetic, sketching stones and placing them in the weedy garden in Bromley common. Yet much later after moving to Thanet, the strangest voice I ever had was when I heard a latching deep pitch and a minotaur with horns in the form of a Prussian black shadow, and I had to look up in the dictionary to decipher the meaning of the sentence, in the Hailey hotel in Herne bay, it said 'you are a prefect of the devil' and then I found out that prefect meant like a schooling, but I twisted it out of fear that it meant I could leave the human-class of egoism anytime without following any darkness.

I guess any darkness I ever used was kind of a shock-reactive act when ill, I kind of sensitivity, that I am a soaker of all the ecstasies and negatives of life, mainly paranoiac reactions in the past lead me to confinement in hospital and by non-confidence, and collective voices.

I joined up with the theosophical society of English in Holborn in 2002 or 3, where I went to a book opening and purchased a copy of the esoteric science by Rudolf Steiner. My opinion from it is that every religion is a path to the same door, and that karma exists, and all religious texts are like riddles to the ultimate Buddhist-like truth that we merely reincarnate genetically and spiritual, advancing throughout lives, and then when perfected, we reach a god-like decision. Spiritual evolution, and I know-this, this is why I do not follow any particular region of the esoteric; I call it the study or realisation off essence-hood, the totality of all. And creativity is its instrument, like protein or Thai-chi for the soul.

When I where sectioned fasted, at first, but then the medication had always been a problem until I found one with the least amount of side effects that didn't make me weight-gain, a little empty, but I battled that. In this book I have included poems, that are symbolic yet sensational for me, and if I believe they are deeply rooted in ageless thinking or my creative struggle.

Section One

Luca WM Blood

This alien steam

beyond the fingerprint skull,
the chapel shrouded in the porridge like- fog,
with one arm a burnt mussel whipping it like cream
coughing dead enemy stealing the tears from the
dream,
in my head little graves,
in each a barking lemon eyed lantern stroller,
as I march, the sepia-tic reel
of a town id left, the chapel moves,
the hairs of grass behind are grey
and are electric mutilated necks.
I've come to the tsunami of love
the hate bearing all woman,
as I put on my skull's glove,
they hack my mind into little pieces of lemon.

Indigo from my vital positivity

sink with the faces in the drips,
waxing of the slowly spinning hips,
her hips, grew, evil, like
the last laugh of a ripped fin,
the grunt of my age behind a handsome face,
draining in a sink,
like a head trying to make balance
to see above the rim,
before the neck blood pales n' slips him,
trying catch the flickering eye of
this sinureta's fancied glance,
as the pupils turn red, like
a light in a dark room,
memories of the castle in bonaffacio,
napoleons cannons,
in the venetian cake brain,
it thinks of the cannon,
it's head being shot through the civil
stars of the Corsican coast,
instead of dyeing in a white minimal sink,
i go back to the womb, the size if my head back
then after i was dead,,
and the hanging heroin of this
thoughtless vent,
where, emotions are more like
aviators, brewing on the
sweet ocean of
mothers heart,
of even universes heart,.
the visions, of trench 85,
like i just came from a life,

Papyrus of the Pillow

where bullets drew vessels,
in that trench where I closed down,
and the atoms of something spiritual,
even to the brutal blows something beautiful,
my eyelids feel like pita bread,
on a surface of hot African mud stone,
and the lips feel like slugs,
in the air of a Sunday spring morning,
the pond of blood in the sink,
like the warm tub out of the womb
of a first vertigo blink,
and the fading rolling reel
of beautiful whores, flickering
like jurgun rebel films,
or silver plates of Barcelona light,
at midday, hitting the eyes of
me the labelling baby,
I wisp to the soul,
back in around me, and
siren my hermetic spirit
to the moment,
I always lived in the moment,
and made love with the canvas, and sketch the mussel
with something lighter than psychic dust,

Orgy of the cranes

wings of city birds,
with bill feathers and news-reel wings,
and schizophrenic movements,
the porridge air with atmospheres
of events slot in
like sugar specs in pantone,
and there dark sisters,
singing the leaders devilish
psalm,
whilst pulling up
tites,
with embroidered tints,
that have an effect of an execution,
alleys without rims or arrows,
that are designed from
the generation's main wind,
without money to guide you through
town,
you turn to a symbol and explode
like atoms on a Pollock painting,
your name useless,
your talent even more useless,
the poppy pilgrims
that commute from city to city
on a trail of advertisement thoughts,
a cafe with surveillance
on the measured movement
of your eyeballs,
and your clothes you cannot get away from,
the wrong match or field,
then you lose your job and home,

Papyrus of the Pillow

the wrong hair and
your heart spins, like a boat
with no rudder and retarded currents.
life today, culture is its fascism,
racism isn't skin colour any longer,
it is the surreal content of
my mind that is decimated,
life today is a catwalk,
with music as it's manifesto
and designer conversations as it's
certificate,
all i am is a great act,
all people in the right hemisphere,
all me in the left,

Castle of the slow retina

the blue laugh laughed like luffwaffer shells eroded,
from a face of seven jaws,
my canine thoughts sizzled n' sussed,
through a chamber of Ethiopian, volcanic Swiss
doors,
my morning fog seemed elegant,
drink the apostle ale,
through the sax of duke elephant,
the choir wingless tourists,
like soda bubbling in a slag gored carcass,
the beautiful fascist-class, cosmologists,
like lima's mountains on Moorish hydroponic
apparatus,
the long tours here are geographically rootless,
with the Greek shores,
splashing up the back of a indigo- tired tortoise,
whilst the pita-bread cave heated
up my buried still yellow skull,
like corpus hermetic's whipping fan,
on the face of Saturn's gorgeous bowl,
the only choosing force of man.

Papyrus of the pillow

the angels are fierce,
with the juices of Zeus,
from the bed-way of magic arousal,
the erotic tourists flip
through the pillows of my seasonal.
in a dream,
it stained the fragrances of wake,
with the thumbed candles of miss's drake,
a river boat creaking
with sea stench like prawn minestrone,
and the boat thinking
with the oars of charlotte bones,
under the sea the bones where
preserved
fancy my skeleton shining
like a bulb in the jaw of the observed.
but the honey n feathers
of the brain, is what i live for
as for the oils set for the
lamps and the crystal,
the Lucca blood gallery,
radiates my incarnations to it
like a kiss or an Arial.
i use a knew pillow for the night,
and dream of the sap of an beautiful
slut,
drip through my nerves
from a mouth of pure lyrical,
feel the guard merge me in,
and wait for the white nectar,
to halo in.

Millennia crucifix

like pigeons patterns,
gently engraved onto my skin,
the oceans groan,
and spill through city bins,
like oilrigs in the heart
for nuisance and sin,
the scaffolding of the Tunisian dessert,
breaks away the schizophrenic swing,
like doodlebugs
marked on fashions and national kisses,
the melding of renaissance stones,
frown and merge into hoses,
like ghosts of a thought,
Asteroiding through the naval
machines into a nature,
turn tree bark to rudder's on modern cutty sarks.
like buttons on a millennia crucifix
the nail is a neglecting laugh,
and the wood is her craft.
I.

Frosted levers

catacomb crutch-heart
walks though the bishop's maid love-Sark,
jewel of jade with a voice,
from her locks and braids made noise,
a flicker through the nerval cliff,
her whispers gently trained south,
from the vanillery slugs of her mouth
but the ocean whirled,
like a cat with a pearl,
so did the curl, down her strut,
made from toffee and swirls,
ended gently the victorious bumming-around
of days which carried frosted levers.

Major Niles

this clapping on
the triangle of my calamity,
moving in boulders,
that grind the man out of me,
i sit sleuthed like a sloth of sin
and in a silent proof voice cave,
the gun's savage their way in.
the fearsome truck,
turning nice white snow to salty muck,
and the spring sparrow liar, lent
on the trig of my wake,
the smacking comes in half of a wisp,
making my heart Toltec jade,
when my mind already are
canabinoids with extended tissue,
like corals of titan,
in a slab of a butchery to the medicine issue
crisping in a winter of syrup-cigarette tsunamis .
I wait for the great eclipse like a
Fish in front of a door shaped mantis.
like Mayan bowl drips,
the radiance is futile,
and halt for a second of
schizo-less bliss,
that i am connected to
the universes job-centre
Yellow instead of red in my wrists.

This way I cough

I cough like planetary shuffles,
and pluck moth wings
like heaving pyramid stones on
sand-irritated sweaty rope by the tong,
and listen out for the great toe's
and great nail's or even Mandela's of the life-long.
I sense a Spartan, grinding at the teeth, in humid
air basil green,
with his hands like a warrior,
cut to a sharkskin gangster-ish sheen,
I sea the lizards weaving through the hollow
nerves of rocks on the Genovese coast,
read a sign directing my heart,
to the tip-toeing Taliban host,
he tells me of all, and all in essence,
that Islam is higher,
without a whoring and nonsense,
he hammers is hand on a pile of snake basket-
fragranced books,
sending our western crooks
to nuclear mushroom clouds when we cook,
today is the sermon,
I met a young robed tramp called Herman,
patted his foot on a puddle of clay grounded hut,
he handed me a scroll,
and by almighty did i know,
that every little religion
are the decorations
that surround the main glow,
the passage is vast,
I am a creator and grow like big-bangs with sailing
masts,

my sketch scribbled by the vitamin chair,
made a pillow-museum of dream choices
out of an project and a spiral of hair.

Notes 11

By Luca w.m. Sebastian blood (burgess)

Taliban tusks around the quasi-coma atom-less
crane, the salt of the Corsican shores, slap their
hands angst the rocks of the tax-credit marble film
grain, eroding the rustic reels, that crash like
mirrors into Shinto tiles, pausing the clocks of dead
prisons, seeping out the butterflies in quasi-coma
systems. tapping the chest of the orb clerk when
near- the flock of seagulls, and dead-trench-man's
empting from the skull, his getaway soul as he
weaves out the last foot from the totem pole skull."

Note 10

the scrawling cloud brawls' down to its last flapping
door hinge, collapsing wood, and the this gaping
quack, earth not luminous blue, psyche red, like
ghost glue, the cerium of being live is sarcastic,
with this touch-funny pagan plastic,
id crawl around like nails, submarine-long, or titan-
ice massive, my eyes as they stair like static
sensors, of the main-air, thick like white chalk in a
shuttle with rattle-snake- drones and erecting hair.
my fist note on this brutally bronze shun, Greek sun
arousing lip of my piper harmonic hyper.,

This side

The hour brass instrument is lucid,
This silly projection,
of my medicated emptiness,
There are frightened lambs on the heath,
Bonding with the huffing moon,
Ridiculed my Mexican lama's that wonder Inca-
rooms,
There are lamps evoked,
By my esoteric hawks,
My brain ball-berrined; the left and right,
And put to sleep with electrical kites,
A Minotaur optician in the form of
A voice that pretends to be a hallucinatory roman,
Or a speck of dust on the paint smeared carpet is
A fake-god trying to rattle my head with holy toilets,
A suicide in me that cannot happen,
Yet a fishnet inside me that takes them like away
Like green gammon.

Mills,

mills mills, spin, spinning
in the windmill beneath effortless ripples, on edge,
when the filtrated orb leaves the body of tickles.
The cave of arousal,
The erotic memorial,
You'll find me,
Dyeing like a candle,
Exorcising like a oceanic handle,
Never enough trace,
To open doors, like opening wars,
The love-sick spilling into migratory trapdoors,
And leave their smoke behind,
You'll find me,
Spilling potential worlds, half soul, and suns,
Reading this boneless mantra,
To a lifeless load of whorish conservative tsars.,
This alarm,
This passable psalm.

Stroll 5.30

The headlights speared forward,
The oil-rig light
A drift of street debris,
The salivary air gobbling,
And mangled where her tight white shorts,
With holes in them,
For the eyes to frog-Lilli inside them,
The ripping strings of laughs,
The seagulls emerging behind her ,
And chewing gum cars,
With souls inside them,
An old man with a hat of bird stains,
Licking his chip-fork,
A breeze of Russian perfume,
People like dots around a naked bather's waistline.

Willow woman

the posing face,
With or without grace,
In her sun-kissed pupils; thundering like Nazi metal,
Fluttering like Spanish tinsel,
to sink into like a tsunami into a genii bottle,
i cannot dream of her as the chair is too delirious,
Like I am a worm lost in the soldier guts of
Spartacus's dyeing world,
Or a flame inside a ministry of ice, will she see me,
With or without grace?

Near-Greenwich- feat of time

An scapular arm of bronze iron, punching out over
the Thames,
From a machine rusted and bled,
Steamed up acidic in the thick porridge air,
A mass of industrial iron nettles,
Perfumed like moon dust,
Pr a caves chunk of put-out candles,
The oil tar, a nutritious soup for an iron world or
A life-boat for mangled machines,
The thick-cream sky, mirrored on the surfaces
Crawlingly faced gunk,
To hear the spray of aerosol
On metal cranes gently flunked,
Behind the factory,
Modern day hieroglyphs
,are organised there,
Whilst hearing the slow whizz and drip,
In this deserted hermetic fear.

Three arches, painting in three sections of mine;

The last swing

The peachy wine in glass, that burns the heart from the hand of memory, and those fingertips like Moses iron cranes, waves sweep hastily the vibrant sunset of the night, into a murky retch or debt. The arches of hell-esque swap for the arched for arched eyebrows, of the miss-caress, on me that wouldn't rest, in this psychological amphitheatre, in the shrine of crime, I turn to Buddhism and write a doctrine.

Minotaur of Luca Blood

Luca WM Blood

Blood pages

Papyrus of the Pillow

The pillow whore

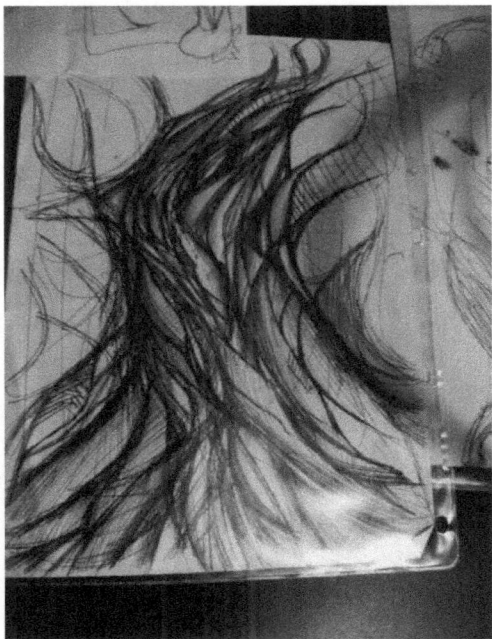

Sketches I produce everyday. Muscular.

Luca WM Blood

Section two

Poems of the papyrus of the pillow

Luca WM Blood

The lost trend

A wide mouth with a vineyard in,
Grapes of the middle-class, rapes of the illumine,
Around I sail my eyes like eggs with fins,
The conversations Ralph Lauren, to voices
Morphed like lungs of a great Greenwich oak,
Watch out; watch out, for the Hyde Park fountain
perverts
As they're armed with jury hammers, and dribble
out liquid policies,
There are bibles growing inside the canary wolf,
Changing around letters into luca's talk,
, like boats on a paper moat,
And the traitor's without necks afloat and alive
Down the Thames's wind pipe,
When i think of communing with the heart's
cancelled,
I'll pluck a moth's wing and do something Newton-
like.

Automatic Reich-
Mathematic with a life

In the phone booth the smoke caved in
The spaces of Ivan to the luminous red of the
Digital Byzantium,
Summoning the youth to use a leaf from a weeping
willow,
Pluck it from a twig, to see my heart rattle,
The tears fell down, like nets from a cutty Sark,
The beers flooded the wooden inns,
Like pulses on my quantum skin,
Firry cherubs reined the stage,
Taking Caravaggio
From his angry Jesuit grave,
Id sizzles to the Toltec sun
I was on stage
When I winked at the zeitgeist Hun,
On a sea of smiles,
When the ghosts of the sky-war's
Filled the sea with hot-cross buns.

In chaplefield noon

The day slushy and empty,
And the ochre night lanky,
In the day of the peach tree with its wet-tong of
blossoms,
And branches like Swiss chocolate,
The grass scribbling it's purplish yellow teeth
And the face in the dirt powdery white,
Like suburban spooks in material sight,
I imagine the titanium blossoms fluttering
Like taxes' through the skeleton
Behind an Yves -Klein blue,
And me lying down on the mossy patio
At the Church's Corsica-shaped feet,
Dreaming of napoleon as a hermetic,
In terracotta heat,
And all the fruits of tranquillity dangling here,
Hallucinating her lavender hands around my chin,
See her white linen and her braided hair,
The Neptune of a kiss.
With one arm pointing to the sky and one leg
tucked in,
Looking like Swiss flakes caped in Greek cream,
Doing the Arabian dance just for me.

The psalm of Luca Blood

I'm throwing back your plastic,
Inside leaping laughs which sing,
To the voice of murky Richmond
With British bridges that burn like white dragons,
Along with stains with the fresh snow of the pole,
Melting away like Byzantium poles,
And vertical skies which rip like nails
Through twilight of grey and white chalkboard nail scrapings,
In the spectacle of the last hermetic.
the luca blood- every ism,
the luca blood- wordless ism
the luca blood- spectrum
the luca blood- making
the luca blood- senses,
luca blood- no tenses
luca blood- no fences
luca blood- fingerprints,
luca blood- anti-analytical
luca blood- essence
luca blood- erotic perfume maker,
luca blood- diagnosis unknown,
luca blood- volcanic jazz,
luca blood- the trapdoor rabbi,
luca blood- system-less Nazi,
the momentary spoon,
Mask-man june,
luca blood- in the carriage,
luca blood- prams of the lost language,
luca blood- a human freeing,
luca blood- viaducts in my being,
luca blood- nation-less

Papyrus of the Pillow

The faceless Sheppard
The hermetic optician,
a string of the twelve division.

The poem of sacrifice

the three reefs, and the carnivorous
belief,
the known soul,
the colours festered
on the totem pole,
away from the death toile,
back to militia, scar-wind,
irritation the tsar of swings,
the Para-kite, Para night,
invisible horseman,
in a brawling 1930's fight,
back down Sainsbury's hill,
the wood piper, plays under lamp light,
warring Martian tides,
with rhubarb soup from an industrial
train freight,
somewhere in pettswood,
living momentary with a liver freight.

Note eleven

Taliban tusks around the quasi-coma atom- less
crane, the salt of the Corsican shores, slap their
hands angst the rocks of the tax-credit marble film
grain, eroding the rustic reels, that crash like
mirrors into Shinto tiles, pausing the clocks of dead
prisons, seeping out the butterflies in quasi-coma
systems. tapping the chest of the orb clerk when
near- the flock of seagulls, and dead-trench-man's
empting from the skull, his getaway soul as he
weaves out the last foot from the totem pole skull."

Note triangle

psyche red, like ghost glue, the serum of being live
is sarcastic, with this touch-funny pagan plastic,
id crawl around like nails, submarine-long, or titan-
ice massive, my eyes as they stair like static
sensors, of the main-air, thick like white chalk in a
shuttle with rattle-snake- drones and erecting hair.
My fist note on this brutally bronze shun, Greek sun
arousing lip of my piper harmonic hyper., the
scrawling cloud brawls down to its last flapping
door hinge, collapsing wood, and the this gaping
quake, earth not luminous blue

Her breathe

A sinking cloud near me,
it morphs into medusa,
The hate bearing all women,
Hacking my brain into pieces of lemon,
The sinking cloud with breasts like vanilla ice-
cream,
And tears like tampon,
my savoir lies in zest,
Where angels treat me like sand
Sculpted by breathe,
Yes I stay alive,
Alive like a curtain,
And awake in this morbid mess,
Now I am contemplating my lover,
Who never came and sleeping
i must sleep with a dream
Willowed like coral above,
Fat with a certain address,
The death bridge from a dream
To death,
The dream,
Caped in thought-free cream.

The ruin

The ruin, ruin of earache,
My ears firing with fire crystals,
My nerves like mammoths on the road to a cliff,
Your heart away from mine,
Will merge like two noses in the same wine,
Will kiss like two kamikazes in the same shrine,
Your smile glowing like nectars in a honeycomb
shine,
Will ruin earache, will climb and gather bate,
And get devoured by peeping Trojans,
Will sit in the watery architecture,
And kiss like brushes in a futurist film protector,
That cuts us a cake like a totem,
And seas shall be aroused by us,
Whilst people are emulsified with the English
grump,
And together lets flamenco,
Dance together thiy by thiy, lip to lip, eye to eye,
Forehead to forehead, over the silly-hills and silly
equators,
Over mills and shells,
Over death and the rest,
Even over the feathery sensation,
Will leave a lucid smudge, stronger than sulphuric
lurid,
You my lover
Kissing like Cleopatra on Transylvanian acid.

Love is drying oil

You love me; i know by spiritual heart,
You dig little tombs in the abyss of my skull and
laugh,
I adore you like roman bathe steam,
And then you vanish like gas into an exit-less
dream,
A riddle and game is always wheeling in,
Through the day I can see our bond blunting,

Claudia's eyes

Claudia's eyes like a still ocean with floating
Piezoelectric lanterns,
Her smile like a boat on a of Himalayan fountain,
She where the earthly right,
Induces euphoria with cannibalistic bites,
Turns a disease into a tiny itch,
She wore green with purple tints,
Here her eyebrow
Like Egyptian boomerangs,
Lips like Turkish delights to touch,
Soft in the light,
She wavered her dress along a pink blossomed
road,
In chapel gate,
She took me to north London on a muddy night,
We had honeycomb servants made of light,
And lime-soda's
Claudia, like a soft
Cushion to dribble on.
Her breathe like Greek air off the shuttle
To the island fair,
Like a breeze in the viaduct
Than connects heart to soul,
And mind to spirit,
Her cheek bones like oriental maids,
Claudia with Aztec braids.

In the space of seven breathes

'Tribute to the great Francis Bacon'

The tears like hot metal,
The hand like light feathers in a boiling kettle,
The revenge like onions to the gristle,
The attack like a sudden Olympic whistle,
His membrane swift as a Shinto swing,
The grains in his eyes like malt volcanic flapping
wings,
The gory leafed group chose him,
Arrogant on the sepia liquid of beery hymens,
In pathetic pubs that witches think in,
But the soldiering wino's spiralled to the politician
jaw,
The mask man flashed like nuclear mountains
vanishing a seesaw,
Like violin strings whipping around them,
His movements had the impact of sand grains,
He splashed them with the power of a dead pale
army,
From wounds Jurassic green the blood flowed
Like blood into wine,
For him to drink the revenge became shield from
The swine.

Lemonchello liquor session

The sheeted white door flapping near the dead fish
toiletry,
Tired cranes with no availability,
A ravage of a thousand jaws on the Ghandi of my
tandoori-red dunes,
A climb up the voice meter,
My fingertips as they tap with retaliation,
Brutal snooker maundering woman with traitor-gate
eyes
And flesh eating judos smiles
Savaging their anti-Zen breezes into my war,
Then I switch prophetically,
Like young Herman on a slide to the silly,
Or a bunker-architect
In a volcanic hazard zone
With nothing but Turkish clay
And an ambient Pompeii bone.

Listening to Shubert

The breezing in the area
Exit tsunamis with pollen
Gently flunked like Negro's bawling,
Elephant Trunks filled with many secrets,
Like black holes or portals
On the skin
The hermetic times fin through,
My stance like a bust
Of xochipilli or
And my expression
Towering like Aristippus of Cyrene
Order-less zest,
In this yoke nutrition for the mussels of spirit,
Down anaconda wind-ways, past cliffy eye dust
busters,
on an octopus heart sensors, to watch what i think

Bloodied dream

The night for urchins
To rip and stomp through,
For pilgrims and strollers
To hurl abuse to,
The black night with
Spines of neurosis,
The whore with an eye
Of wilted bosses to weak
To keep their clubs on four horses,
The gloss maids with violent noses,
Choking the gushing mud
Out of the little outsider who reads Zion proses,
They slam down their skirted cocktails,
And move like monsters making me pale,
They rip testicles like prawns,
With their medieval nails,
England oh England the nights of the angry yawn,

When the attacks begin
My third-eye will dilate,
Phone dials will quantum and turn
NHS pharmacologists into seventh sense bate,
I'll be thrusting bronze jugs into the hairy air,
With Dionysus with Herman with German war lords,
With deities with Ivan's with samurai's perched
above doors
With Taliban tyrants and Spartan artillery
designers,
With a Lilli on both cheeks,
Prams of fire and
Moons wood-pecked to death,
Lambs communing with the messiahs

Papyrus of the Pillow

And queens under aboriginal-neon-red tiers,
Pigs turned to the sky
Leaving graves for the man
And welcomed with shuttles,
Fish will evolve into watery humans,
Whilst politicians are lashed by Martian al-Qaida'
giants,
The slaves from titan building bridges with ice-like
orb,
Towering like vertigo, pulling rope with
Their antelope hands,
The sands of Saturn
Making a mafia Out of these hands.

Zara the tsar

Zara's eyes where
Ball bearings rotating
Ghostly shuttle aluminium,
and dripping...
Away little mirrors into erotic museums,
My ego-ape side, chalk graffiti
In each reel of her vivisecting memory,
The reel phased out,
Id graph down doodles into the planet of her hips,
My buzz-holy poses sealed deep within her wrists,
Slush' slush' the tangerines of drive squished,
My buffering testicles,
Set like life-rings on her sea adrift,
Testicle like an eye equal to the green tint
In her lucid telling right eye,
As she focuses on the puff
Of black rings coming from my glittered white lie,
Her aiding cuddly stuff,
A parlour for the dream,
Her presence, like
Venetian sun sheen.
Like Tongs on the testicles
Turing My fruity vineyard
Into a barrack of
Abandoned wedding rings.

Doctrine

To hear words those aren't mine,
To know how luminous
These dust and scratches are in
The projector of my mind,
A mere musk filled and masked shadow theatre,
With hallucinatory Gestapo
I sit in this psychological amphitheatre
To me a self-built shrine,
Then I turn to Buddhism,
And write a doctrine.

Love and its fat

Forever there is a fact,
War and violence is in the blood and fat,
In everything it is intact,
I smell into in the strings of sex,
Feel it in the silk of beauty,
And taste it in modern electricity,
The only escape is to leave where you first sat,
Is across the viaduct,
Through death's snoring crack.

Sheppard', Sheppard' we have a problem

The sun like orange glass,
Peel away the masts on oceans for an hour,
So sailors can see,
All the earth's metal and skin foam green,
So the lambs can walk silvery,
In Genoa, as I stand staring at a
Fog of Spartacus,
Its face feels like a draft shooting cave
And the tankard slammers of
Barbarians dead
Deep in the mass graves
Inform me with hawks in clusters,
Heading to the American coast
With spades.

April noon's in pagan rooms

The chitchatting breeze
Rousingly soft and flirting
On me, white blossoms like custard
Delights lisping in the ear of my day,
Ill laugh at Britain's rumple stilt skin mind,
In Malt tranquilly and lie in a Shinto siesta,
Where not an Arian soul could fester,
Because I have nowhere to hide
In the trenches of vanity
Assassinated by a system after system
Of designer sexuality,
And aped on by lad-ish society,
In the great red-bollocks
In the rude stiff lip of Sherlock this England,
Surveillance on
Every atom
And psychic bone of
Passages.

The sulk

I never sulk unless I am
Strapped down by the pharmacological
Garlic's Of the NHS church,
Seeping in like Jurassic malt
Or sap in the doors of
My life palm -wallpapered
Airport, making
Me swot sourly,
I am a mere blood sheep with
The orange sun and the grey slum,
The portraits around the pill-sanctuary
Of a tramp, piping a pipe,
On the newsprint perfumed and oily slabs
Of Thomas Becket's touched ground,
In Canterbury that the civilised barbarians
Still walk around,
I'd wake up like a frosted soul
Scraping its leaves off the bed of black oil,
Like a gun-powdered spider in Arabic soil,
The bells heard a mile away,
From a fashion parade
That useless,
And me with pesto fingertips,
Living on olive oil and canvas strips,
Waiting for a nice bag
of soil-grown chips.

Olive tree

The sky deepened with turquoise blue,
My heart just the same,
The olive tree sitting down
By the grass
With one knee tucked in,
And one arm pointing at the sky,
Olive tree with lime green hair,
It chased away my nightmare,
From the indoor walls which haunt and stare,
By the grass the grey cat strut its tail,
With all its female attitude,
And closed into a ball of soft brown terracotta,
The peach tree danced like an Arabian,
Its Mexican red and orange cheeks,
Its muddy-rifle like branches looking
Like chocolate flakes from an ice-cream,
The mood was somewhat rejoiced,
All earth infused into this meadow,
The turquoise sky that i could peel off
And rub into my skin like moisturiser,
The olive trees that i can skittle
Down my throat to
Make my heart double its chambers,
The flossy green blossoms in all wavelengths,
That where a projection of my
Impulses, like confetti weaving though
A wind of blossoms
My love aloneness,
Like a limestone in a desolate cave
Where shadowy soda-straw figures
Glare at me with fatted sinkhole smiles.

Your black pupils

Shield me from
The bloated wilted cactus, Lucifer,
Grey with horror it
Hacks at my brain like
A demented crane,
Burns in my electrical nerves
Like a reigniting suicide bomb plane,
The devil more than just black,
Like oriental ink blots of bats,
To rid it though the owl of ceiled
Fatherly comfort,
Ill walks away though
Smokey kebab machines and
Medieval cutlery noises
Vibrating into my sleeping lagoon,
Go away this stain,
Splattered like dead moths
You made me turn into humans,
I am Petrified of it;
In this egg-burning presence,
This meat hook clanging twang,
A phonological screech,
That of a sand-timer filled
With Smokey eyelids
And faceless cryptids,
That of a phantom of a tranquiliser,
Demented crane with its haunting perfume,
Ill shake you off,
And you'll return on horseback,
Psychopathic Minotaur,
Awake on a headless bull
With horns larger than canary wolf

On my round like ying yangs,
Anxiety the red sky,
Dexterity the pink flame,

To found out that all started
with the medication
And its little grains.

Random junction

A face pale as pita bread,
The face frail with a lifeless grin,
Laughing at a shadow covered in circumcision skin,
Hunting for glory, the beat several breathes still on,
With a heart more red than tandorri voiced songs,
Its wrong where the pantomime started,
Jack in the box's collected and clownish chavs
hunted,
Randomness of bullet erythematic
And peasant systems gold coated,
Like Jamaican fins in Atlantic ice,
or Somme lead in stomach swamps.

Luca WM Blood

Antiquity of papers

The autistic-ness of business,
Metal squares and logic muted,
Like putty in the lung,
Of scaffolding wrecks in the heart,
The whitening of rain,
The tightening of the brain,
Commuters scurry like
Jumpers from planes,
The citizen who chases the great scurrying mass,
And the wardrobe of dirty dormitories
Catapults the parliament cat flap
 Like snotty socks and suited bats,
The government not my design,
The system a embryo drowned in blue tack,
The way he thinks,
Like byzantine choir group in a sound proof sack.

www.ingramcontent.com/pod-product-compliance
Lightning Source LLC
Chambersburg PA
CBHW031141270326
41931CB00007B/639